The study of the violin presents certain difficulties for beginners which are frequently the cause of a sudden abatement in the pupil's zeal and ambition, even before he has mastered the first rudiments.

The blame for this is commonly laid on the teacher, who is called incapable or negligent; losing sight of the fact that the pupil began his studies without the slightest notion, not merely of the difficulties to be encountered, but also of the regular and assiduous industry indispensable for surmounting them.

It is important, therefore, to smooth these first asperities by showing their utility and making them agreeable; to this end my Violin Method was published and the present Exercises have been written, which latter may be considered as forming a supplement to the former.

If practiced carefully and intelligently, they will serve as a solid foundation for the technique of any player ambitious to become an artist.

Franz Wohlfahrt

No. 1

Allegro Moderato

No. 2

Allegro Moderato

No. 3

Moderato

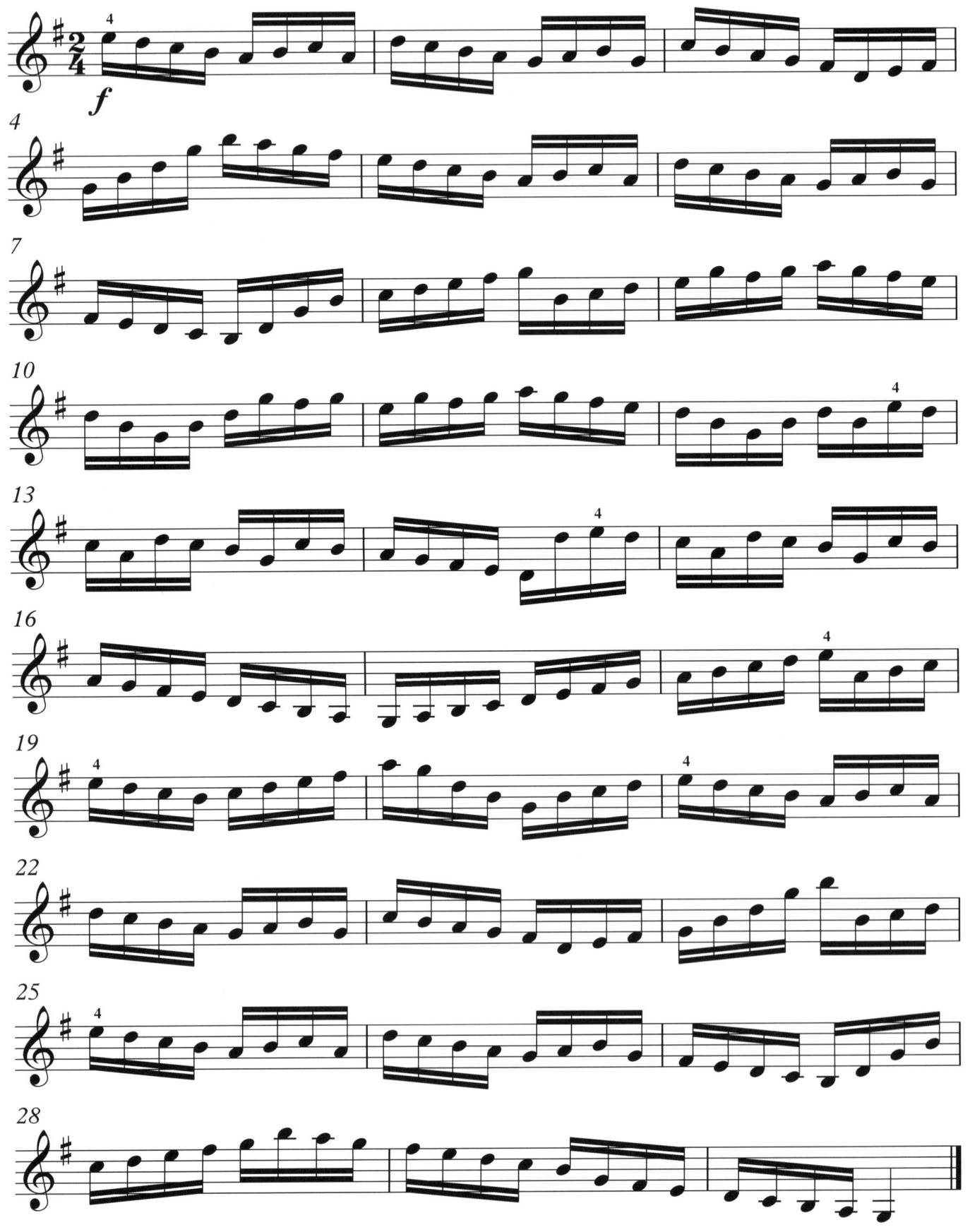

No. 4

Allegretto

No. 5

No. 6

Moderato

No. 7

Allegro Moderato

No. 8

No. 9

Allegretto

No. 10

Moderato

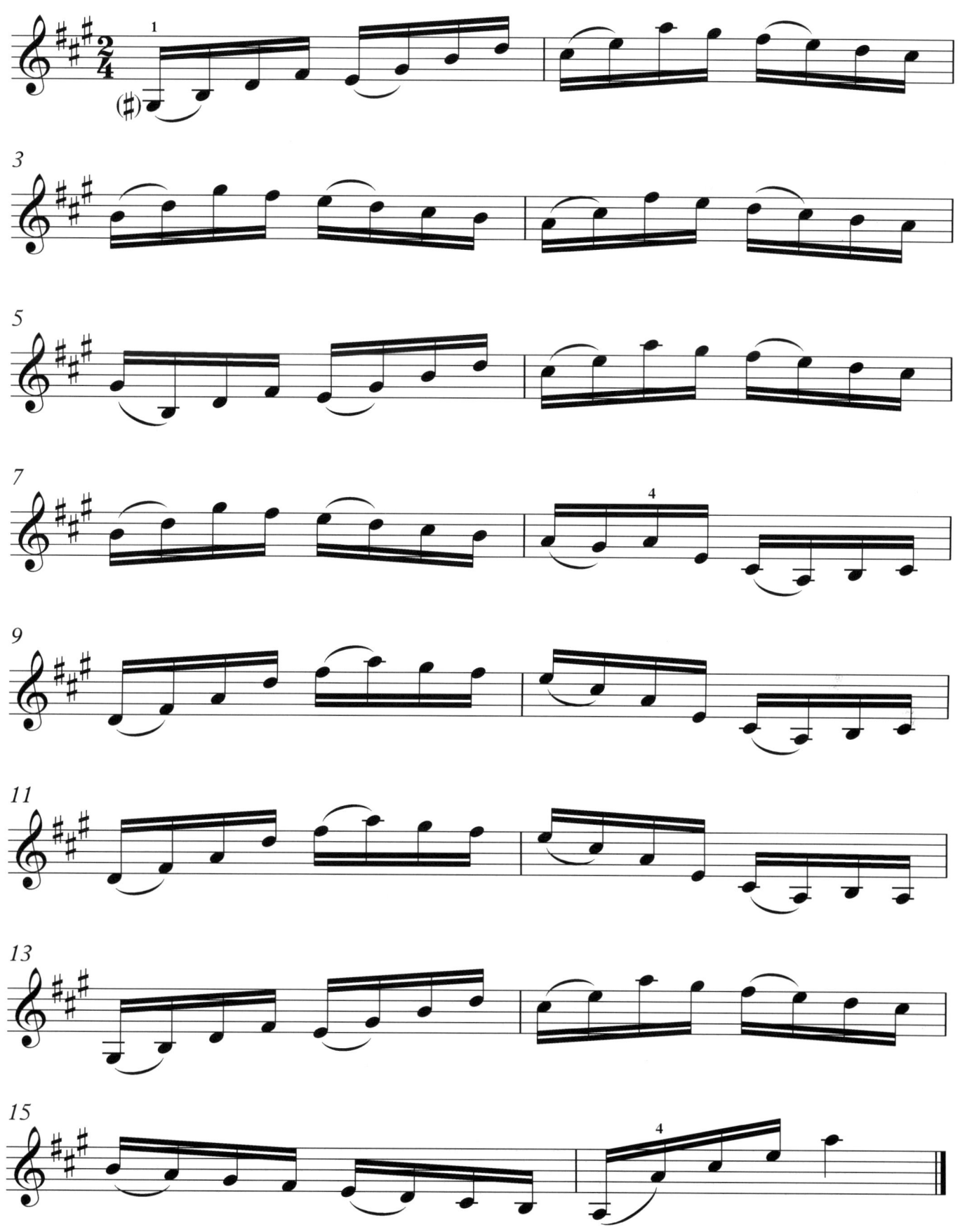

No. 11

Moderato

No. 12

Allegro

No. 13

Moderato

No. 14

Allegro non tanto

No. 15

Allegro

No. 16

Moderato

No. 17

Moderato assai

No. 18

No. 19

Moderato

No. 20

No. 21

Allegro

No. 22

Allegro

No. 23

Moderato

No. 24

Moderato assai

No. 25

No. 26

Allegro

No. 27

No. 28

Allegretto

No. 29

No. 30

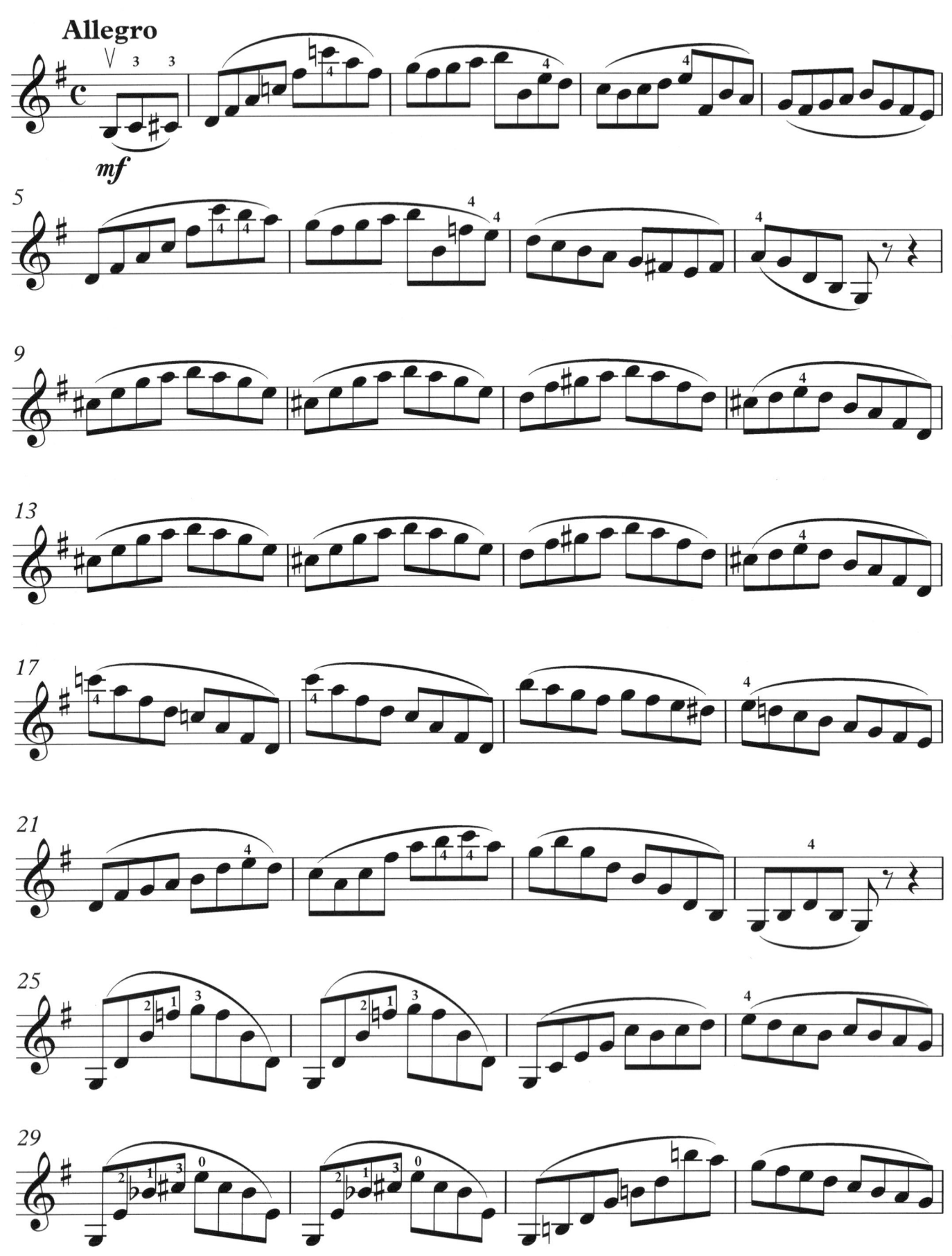

No. 31

Moderato

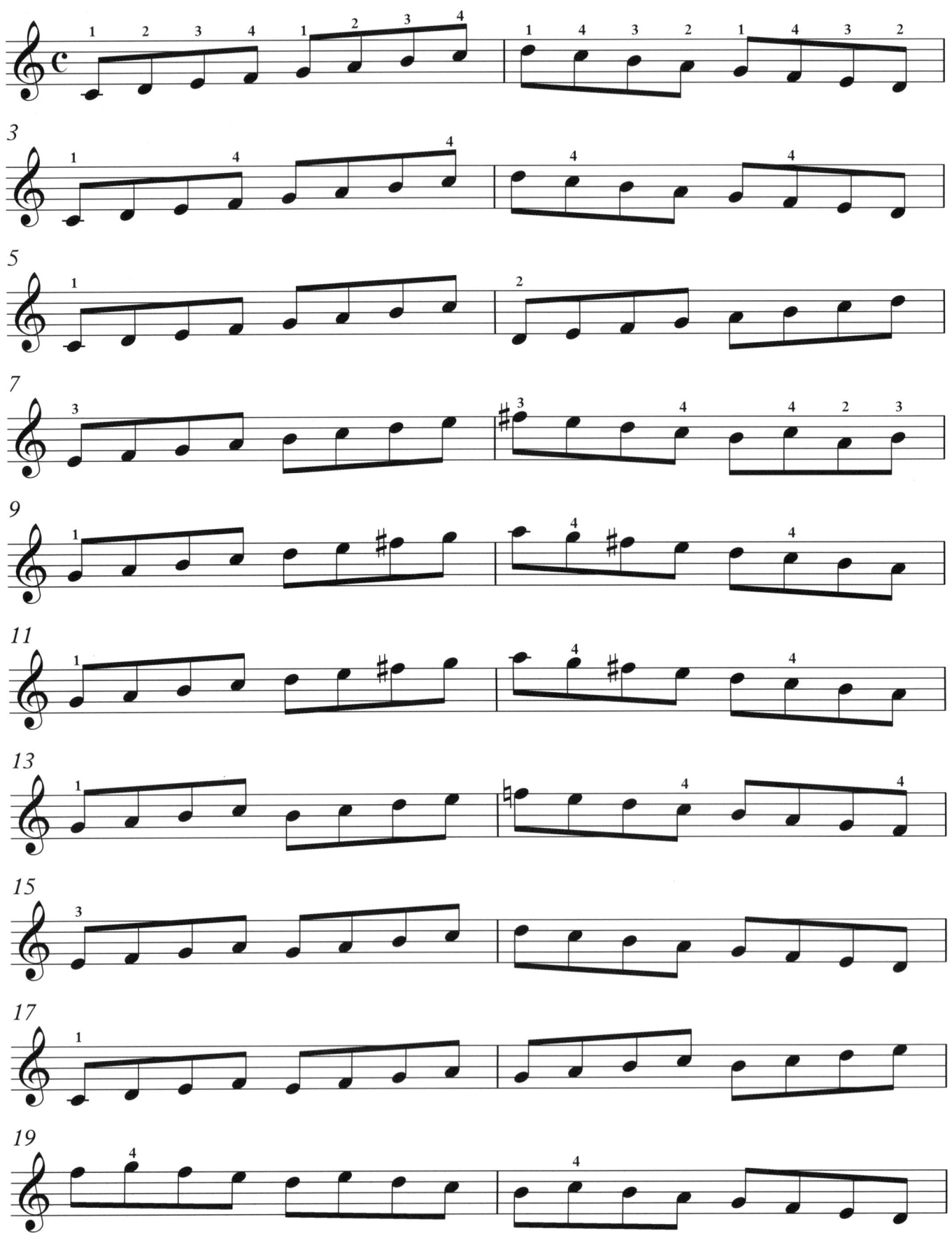

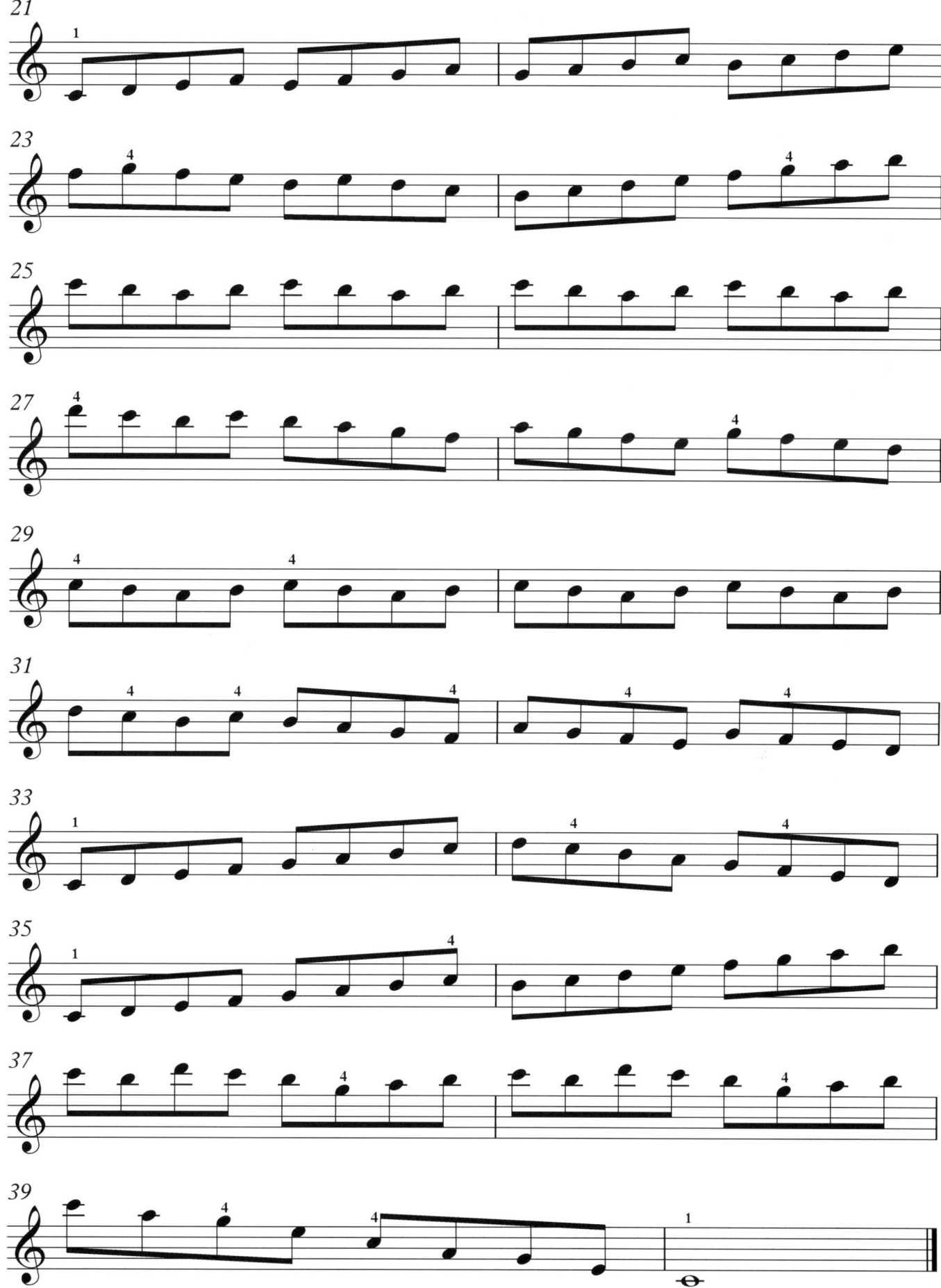

No. 32

Allegro

No. 33

Allegro Moderato

No. 34

Allegro

No. 35

Allegro

No. 36

Moderato

No. 37

Moderato

No. 38

No. 39

Moderato

No. 40

Allegro scherzando

No. 41

Allegro moderato

No. 42

No. 43

Moderato

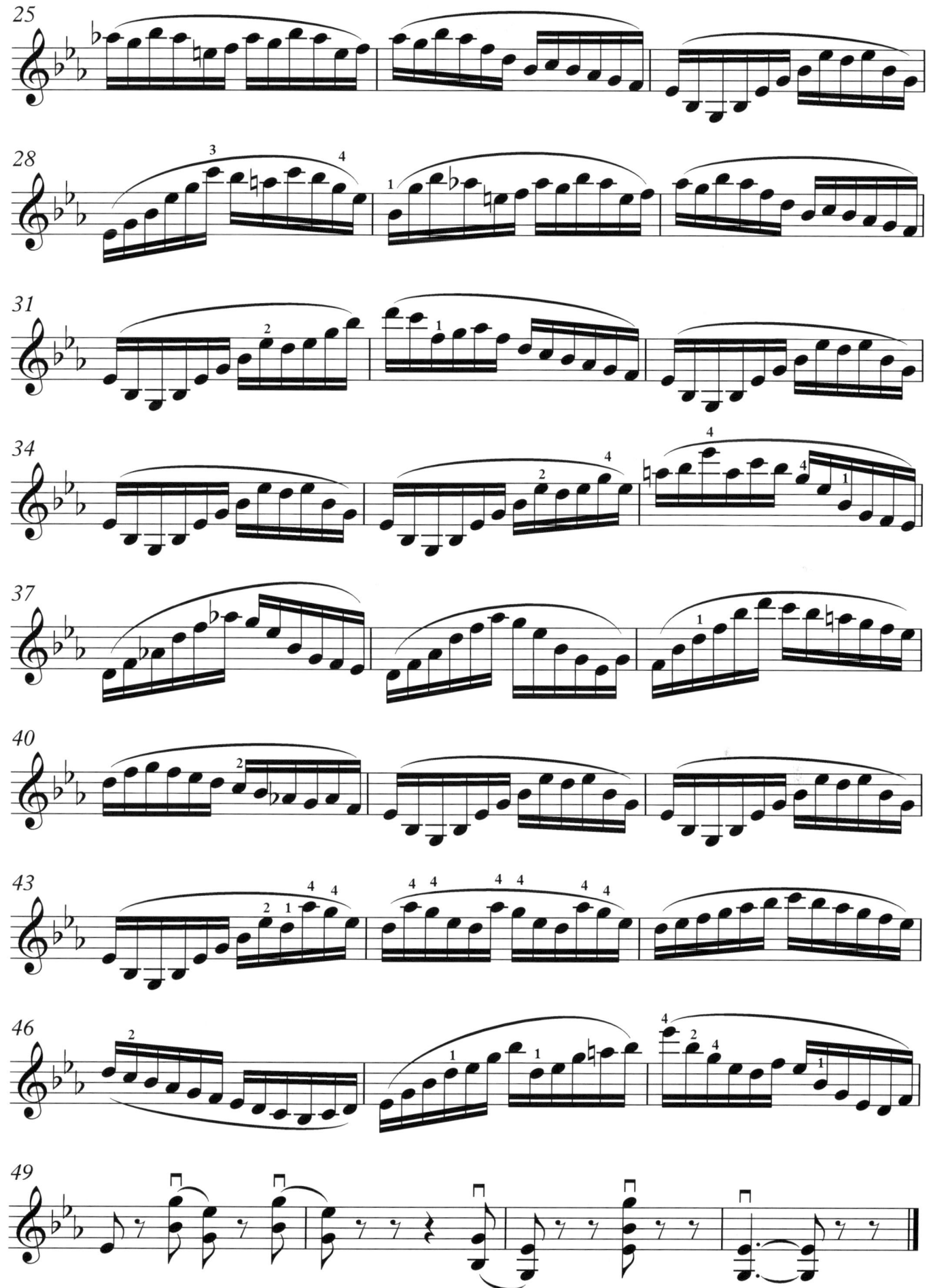

No. 44

Tempo di marcia

No. 45

Moderato

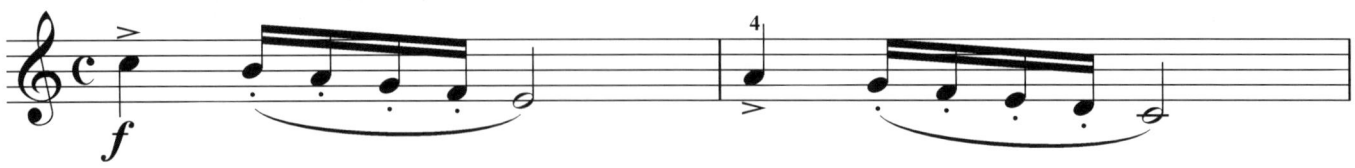

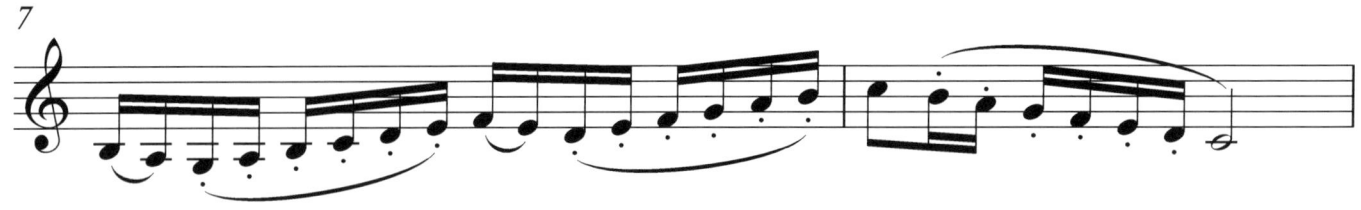

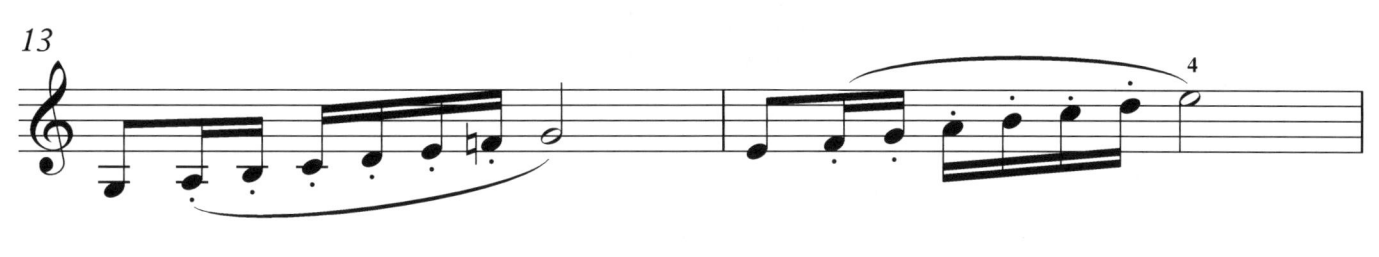

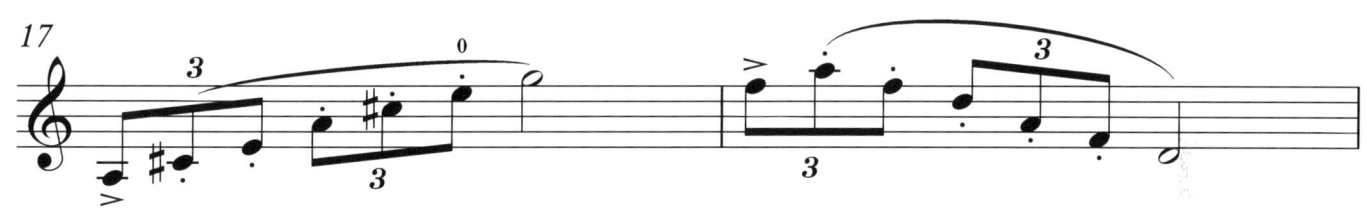
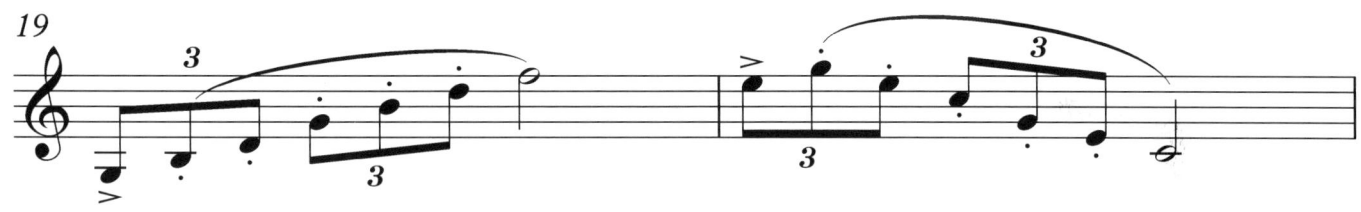
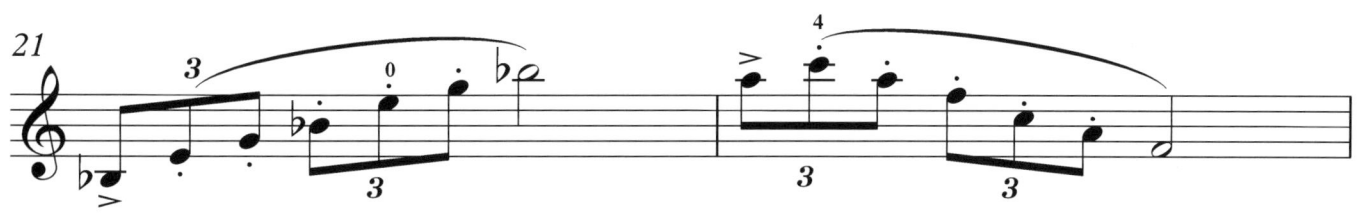
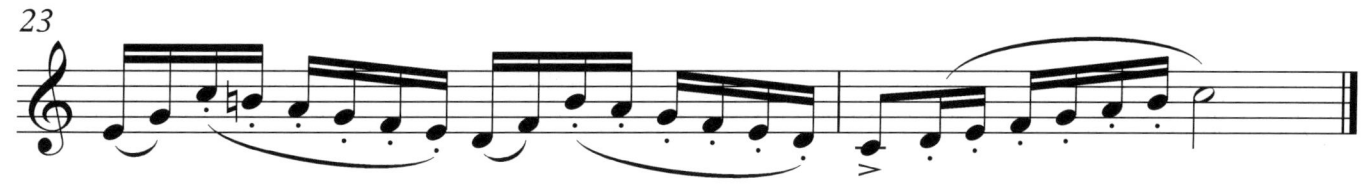

No. 46

Allegro

No. 47

Andante Cantabile

No. 48

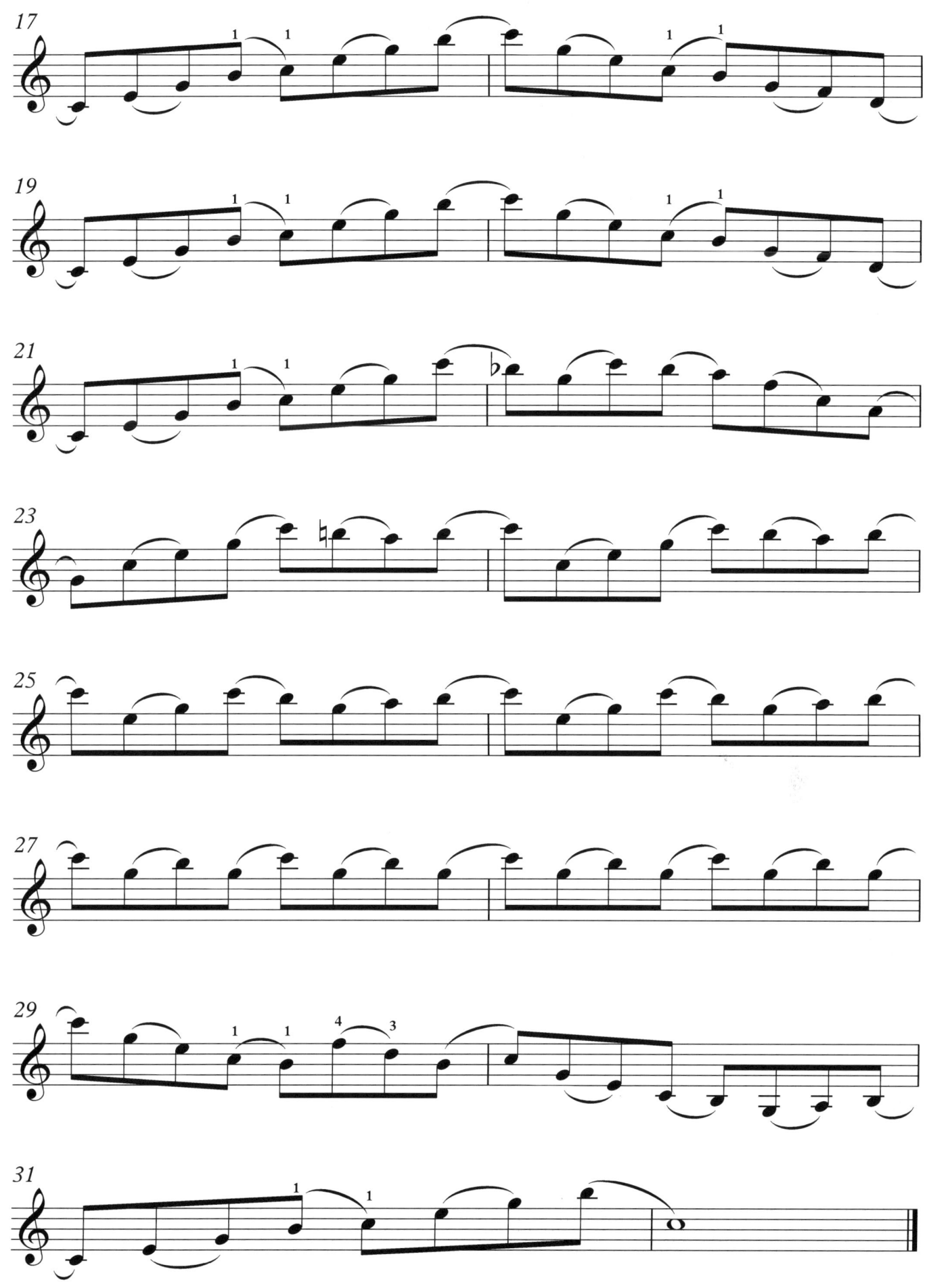

No. 49

Allegro

No. 50

Allegro

No. 51

Moderato

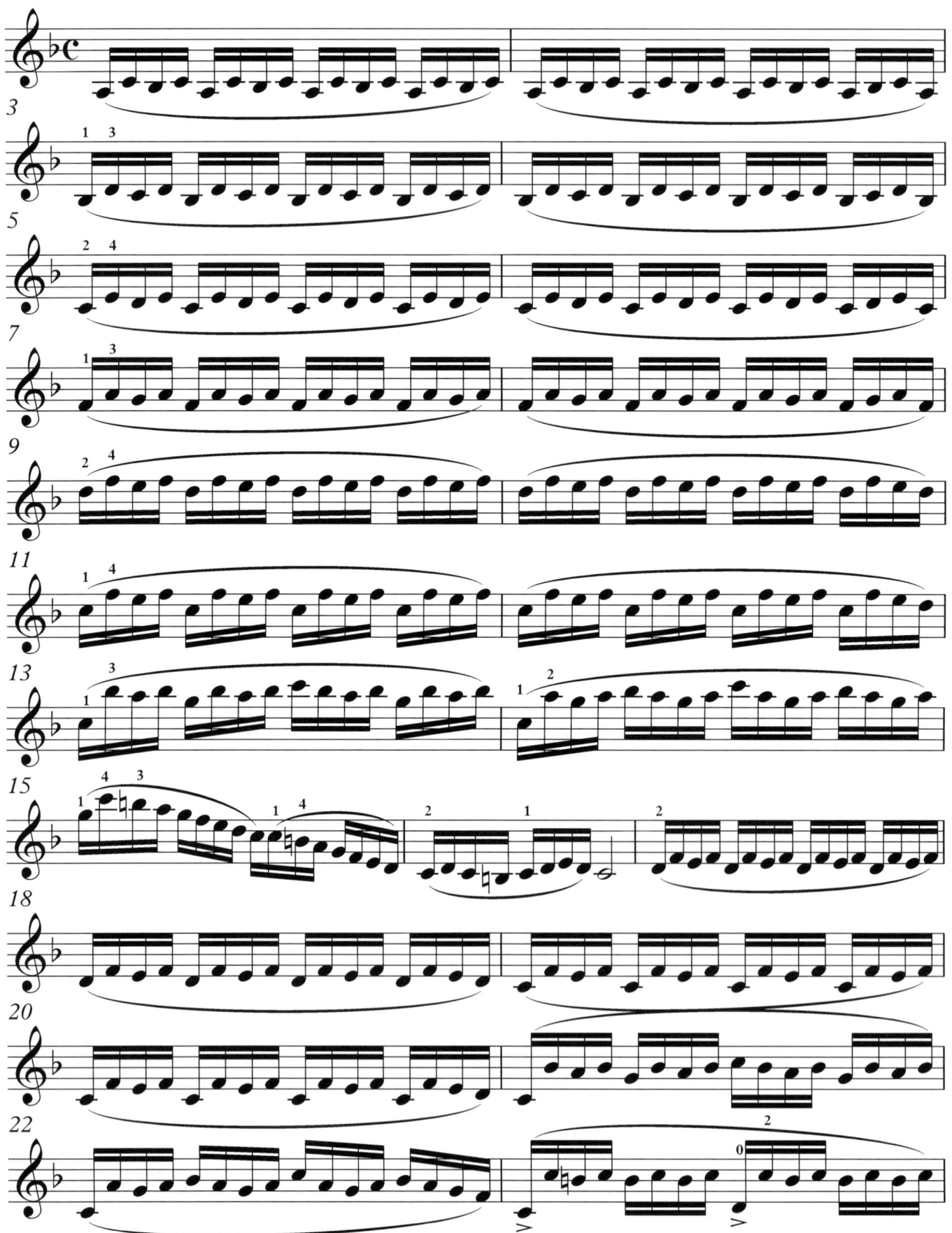

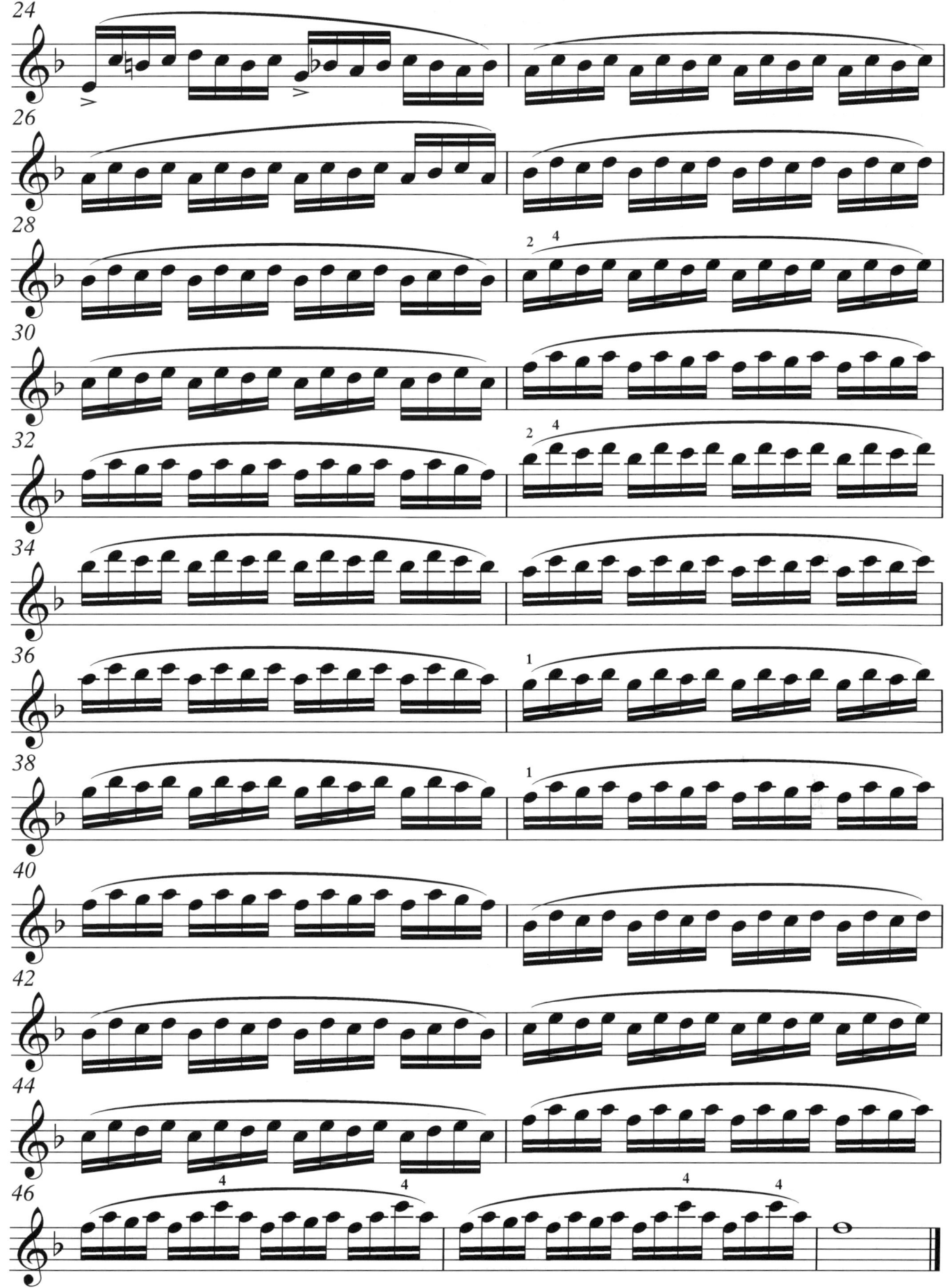

No. 52

Andante

No. 53

Andante

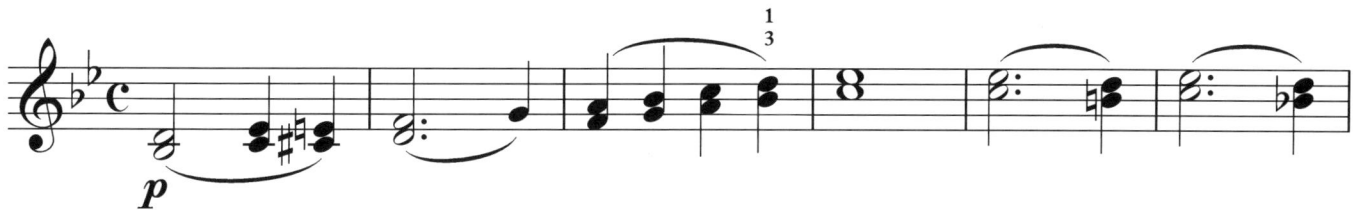
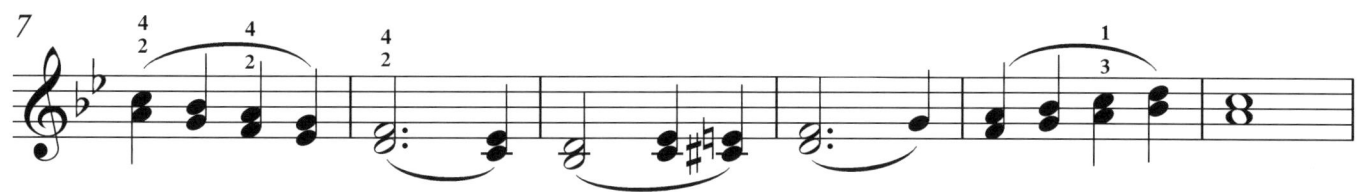
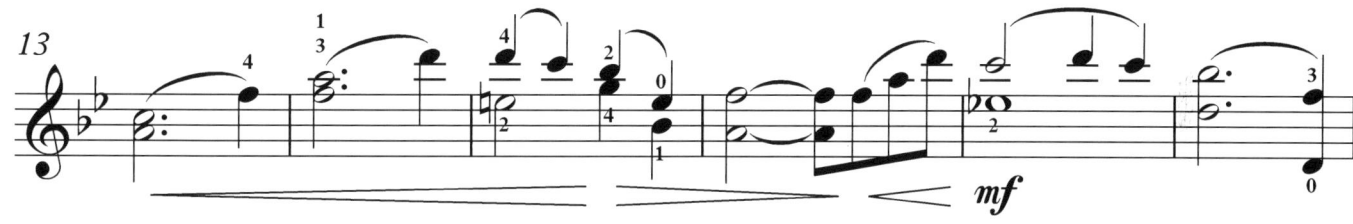
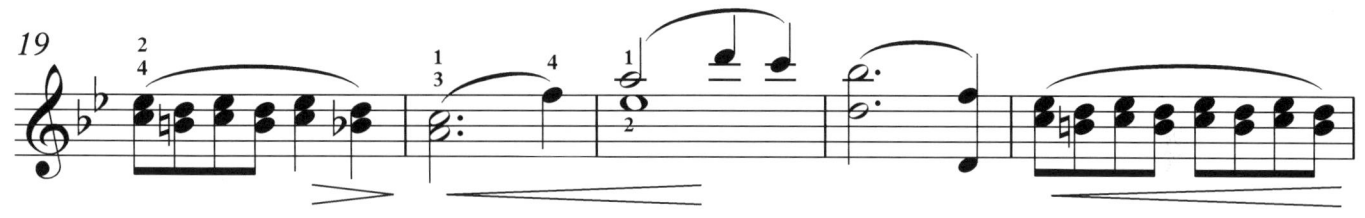
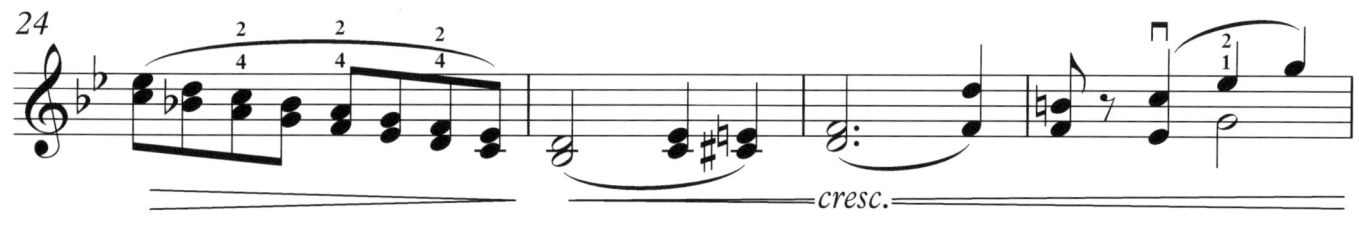

No. 54

Allegro

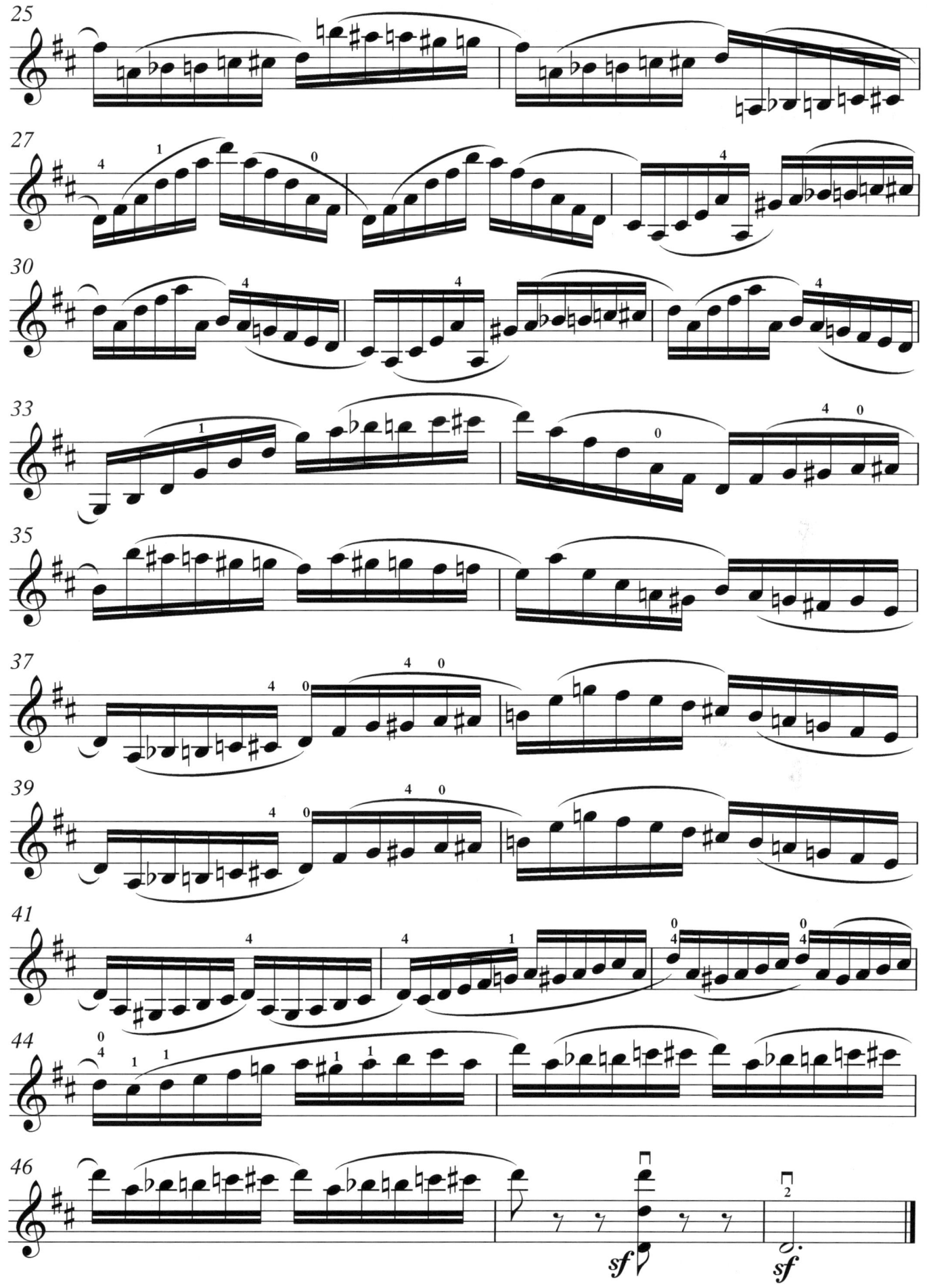

No. 55

Allegro

No. 56

Andante

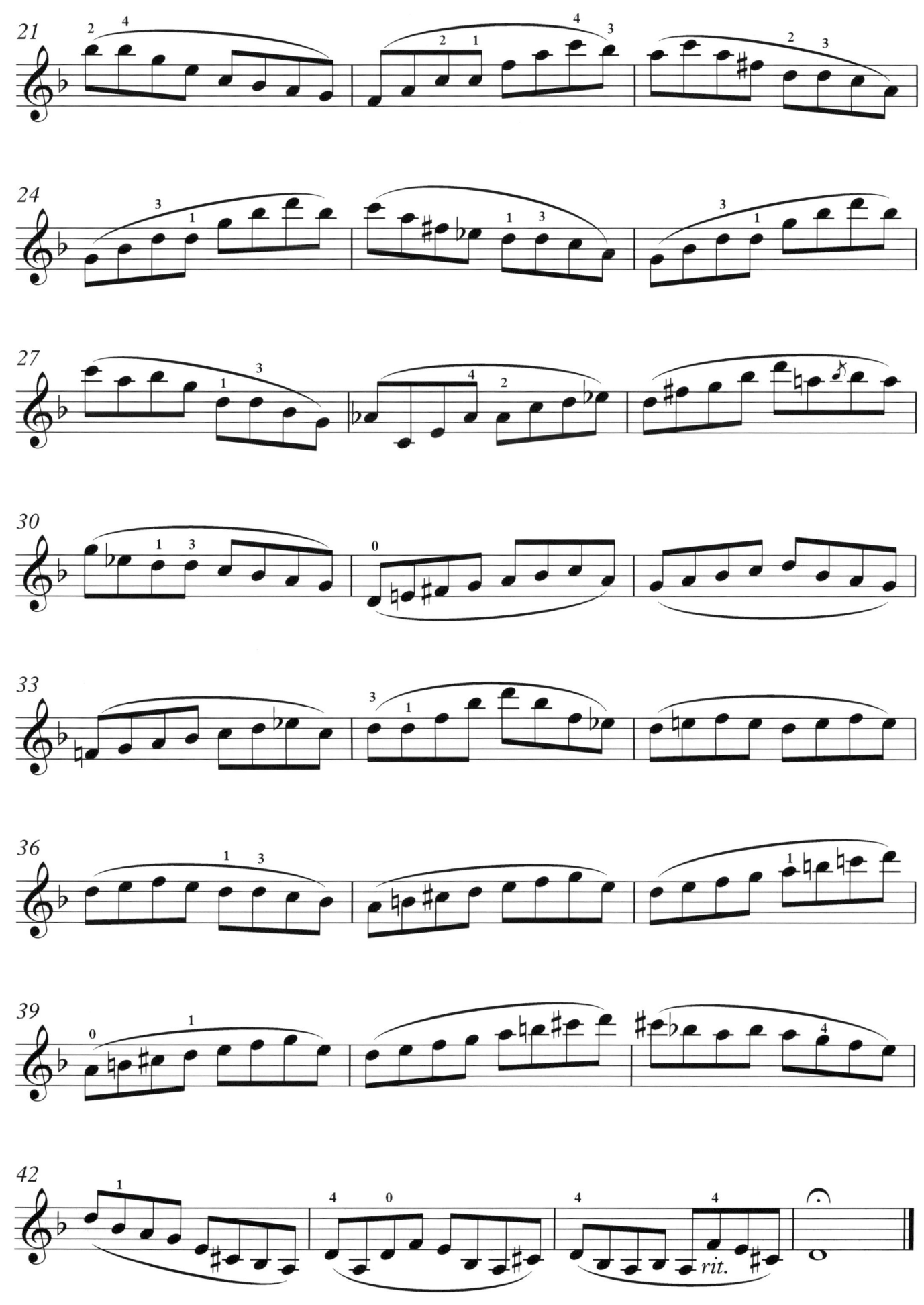

No. 58

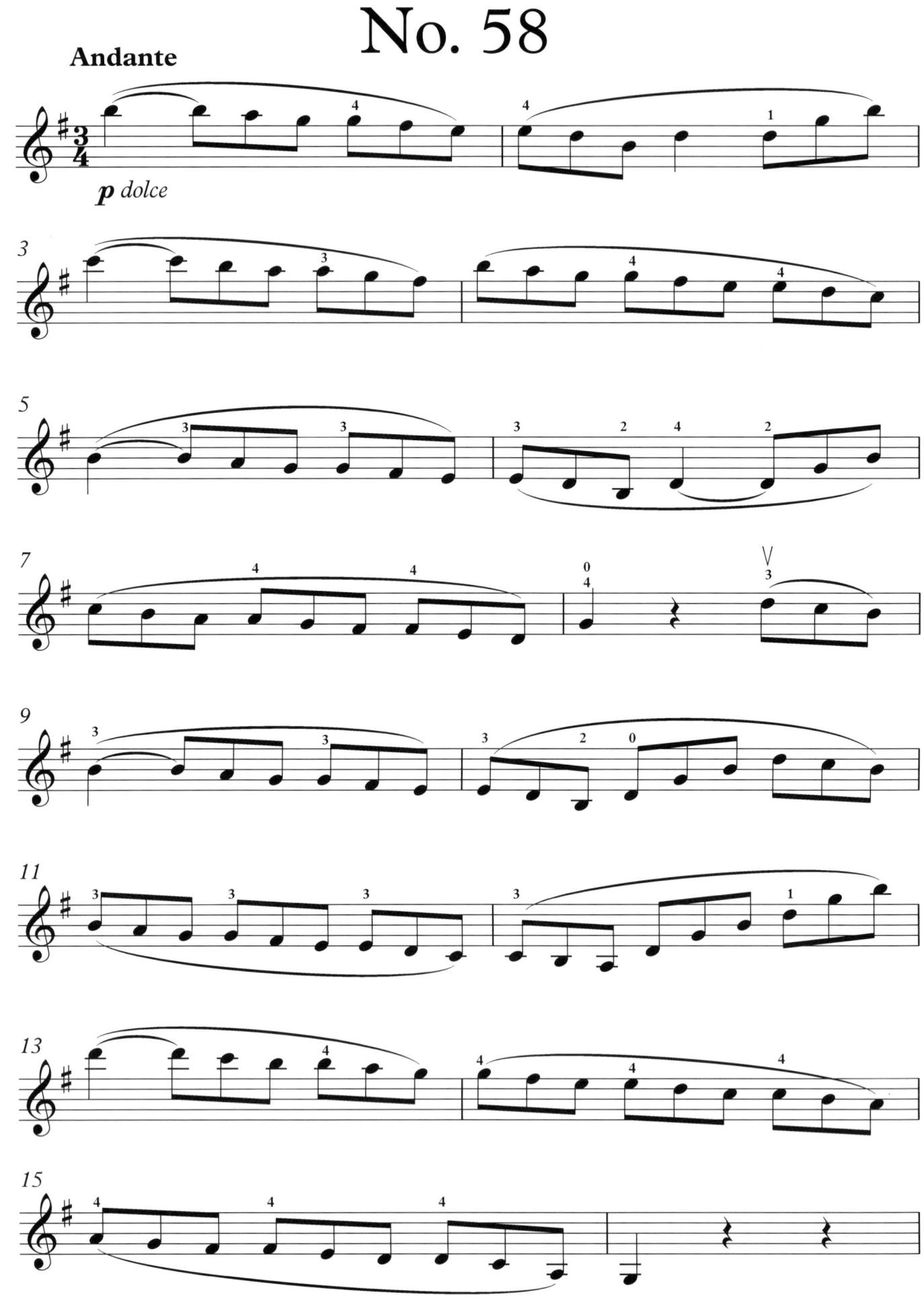

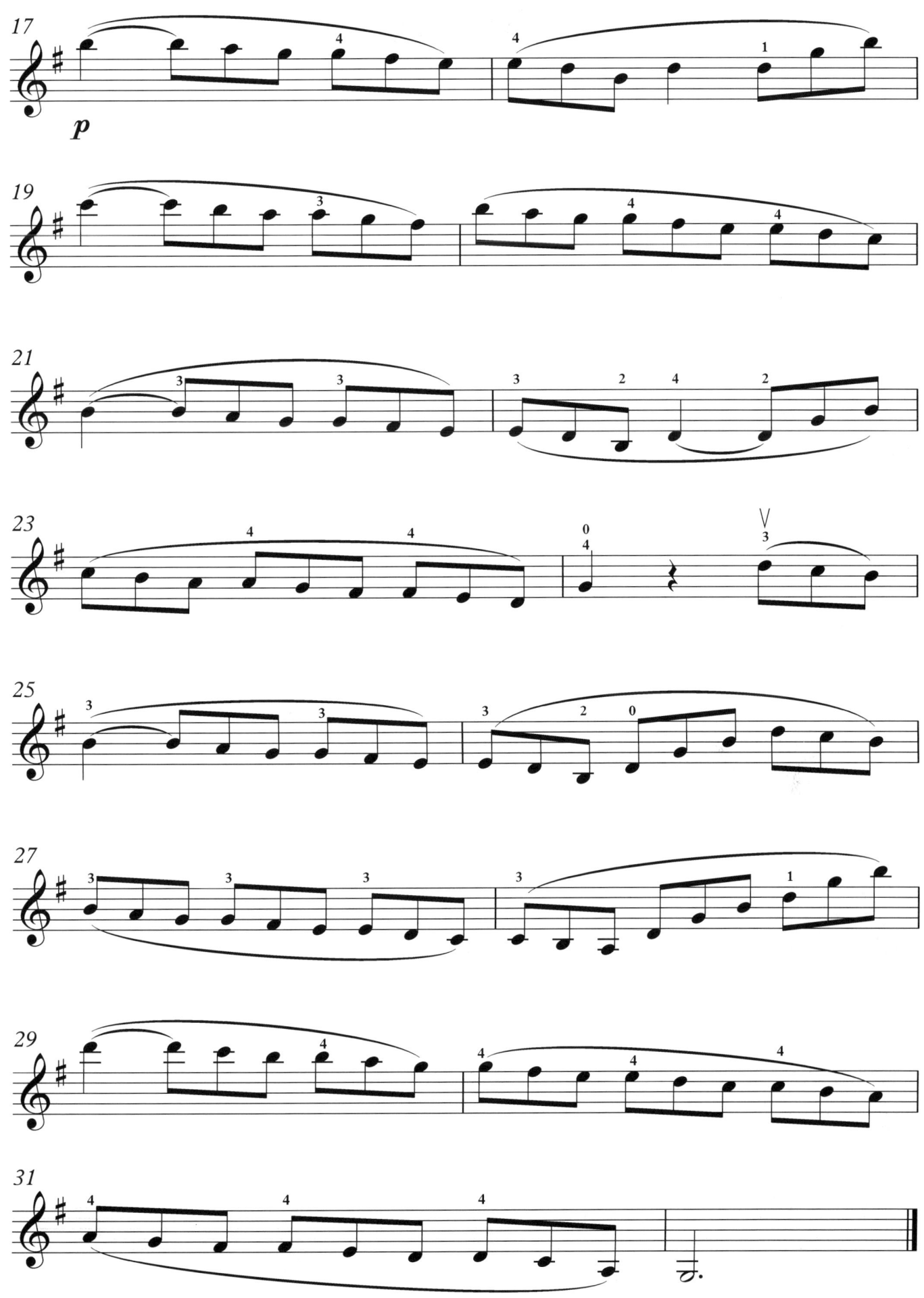

No. 59

Moderato assai

No. 60

Allegro con fuoco

Made in the USA
Columbia, SC
25 July 2017